Beneath the Shadow of a White Pigeon

A Collection of Poems Composed By
Pijush Kanti Deb

Happily dedicated to my Heavenly Souls, to my Sitala Maa,

And to my earthly readers.

As well as to my Gurudev and my Father.

Broken Pitchers

Bearing the brunt of betrayal of
someone we love and care for
fills the pools of my eyes with tears
and the whole world sinks
in to the depth of black brine
yet it makes them quite transparent,
tearful eye witness
bearing their lot of grudges
against our true love and affection.
Before we are convinced
they beat a selfish retreat from us,
leaving us alone
in the maze of thrones of confusion
to put two and two together on the query
"Why do they bear us hard?"
Maybe, unabated beating of our brains
will bear one day fruit for us,
colourful, fresher fruit will be available
to refresh us,
new hands will keep company
with our old hearts to remold them.
Alas! All will be in vain,
as broken pitchers can never be adjoined again.

To Read A Brand New Book

The old reason and the young desire
call for a whispering conflict
regarding an appropriate time
to read a brand new book,
unwrapping it carefully
by eager fingers,
looking at the beautiful paintings and stories-
painted and written skillfully
by a well known painter and writer,
by the enchanted eyes.
They start casting of arrows of
arguments and counter arguments
to each other
till the casting of the last arrow
and at last,
a cartel- the gainful last resort
appears between
the most powerful and ever- agitated rivals-
mind and brain,
decides- a noon-hot and matured,
the appropriate time to open and read
the book with entire satisfaction.
Alas!
On the hint of the restless heart
the foolish eyes welcome
the abrupt flow of wind to fly into the room
from the impatient world
through the open window.
It comes in and starts playing
" Go as you like" with the immature reader
trespassing each and every corner
and finally ensnares the reader
to make the book opened, naked and read.
Within a fraction of a moment
the virginity of the book is lost,
reader's immaturity and ill-competency are detected
and the most thrilling earthly pleasure is left unfelt.

An Intermingling Between Ocean and Desert

The world witnesses the same case
happened to two lives-
beloved inferior and neglected superior
along with its ocean and desert
when
a cat suffers from a delivery pain
lying on the heap of money and jewels
making the rich bungalow tumultuous
in extending helping hands.
Call the doctors!
Inform the photographers!
Invite the press!
An oral hustle and bustle
starts reverberating in the separated air,
and within a fraction of a moment
a few flocks of money
start flying out of the bungalow.

At the same time,
not so far away,
just in the backyard of the bungalow
a poor hut witnesses
a groaning woman, restless in delivery pain
lying on a heap of dirty rags.
Just forget the photographers or the press,
even no money at all
to call a doctor.
Time stops here running,
protruding its eyes
to the screaming woman in pain
and then joins at the prayer
conducted by the family members,
begging the blessings of the God
for healing the pain of the woman.
The witnessing world looks ashamed
and thoughtful in planning to have
an intermingling between ocean and desert.

An Avatar- An earthly incarnation of the God

The compelled present gives
neither false coloring to its faded painting,
nor falls out with the so-called painters
and the clotted layers of time on the painting.
The painting,
painted on the old canvas of history,
quite magnificently and beautifully
with mysterious skill,
went a long way in winning
the eyes, heart and soul of the universe
during each and every revolution of the sun.

Alas! Present looks quite blank and blue,
exhaling its grief for the dying painting
and the flying away of its well knitted dream
but hopeful always
as each and every sunrise waits for an Avatar-
the earthly incarnation of God,
with a thorny broom in His hand
to sweep the dirt out of his beloved painting.
Maybe, blood-shedding and hustle and bustle-
the side effects of sweeping,
tremble the body, mind and soul of the witnessing present.

The Biting Soul

A dogmatic life longs to be on the floor
to dance on the rhythm
of a haughty and naughty heart
stimulated by the addition of a keen discernment
in life and heart
along with up-to-date sagacity and black magic,
creating a plain under the table
and tempting pockets to welcome
seas and oceans with their entire treasures
leaving propriety unheard outside the door.
The remaining virtue still peeps for a while,
throws away its useless plumb- line
and joins in the blind man's buff
to allow the shadow of wealth and resources
causing an eclipse on the rules and regulation
provoking the old soul-
made in heaven,
to enter the workshop to make a sharp tooth-set
for its starting of unabated biting
on the soft part of its beloved heart and life
to bring their consciousness back on the right track.

A Duet Song

A sweet piece of duet song
can't set sail for a beach of success
in the elastic ocean of compromise,
heart trembles in fear of sinking
of the sweetness and the appreciation
that a music deserves to own forever.
Neither a gorgeous opera is wanted
nor a reward or a award is expected,
only a normal and sweet duet is longed for
to perform on my common stage
with my beloved- my co-singer
who smiles at my smiling heart
to make me cry in the rehearsal
as she proves to be incompetent and discordant
with my musically trained tune
and makes the duet a noise to the ears.
My compromising hands are outstretched
to match her tune with my tune
climbing one scale up and down by turns
yet the rehearsal breaks up soon
on the harsh ringing of her dogmatic bell
and so no duet is made yet ready to sing.

A Folding Spring

A folding spring is made
to travel forward,
lying, creeping
walking and running
till the opening of all its folds,
and compelled to start
its inevitable return journey
reversing its unpleasant movement
running, walking,,
creeping and lying
till the closing of it all folds off
and it allows itself to disappear in history.

I Surrender To The Tradition

At last, I surrender to the tradition
to live a blissful life
exiling my masculinity-
the culprit of all bitter clashes
in my underarm
and start enjoying the magic
that ensnares my sky, my land
and my beloved belongings
to start dancing and singing around me;
my logical babbling,
rough and tough attitude
and "Do or die"-the powerful hymn
start sneaking from my orbit.
The people,
sad, disturbed, angry and zealous,
owing to my free and harsh masculinity,
start reverse marching to their origin.
The needless eyes
may shut their windows down
yet they witness
the smiling faces, appreciating lips
and helping hands-
ever-ready for nurturing my newborn happiness.
The compromised heart
buys hundreds of charismatic worlds
in exchange for only one: the dogmatic masculinity.

The Stars to be Favourable

Maybe, the raising head
touches moon or mars
and the race between man and God
reaches its competitive climax
in extending or sustaining their own greatness,
yet, something like an extempore speech
or the building of a sweet home
needs oiling the stars to be favorable
in converting the heterogeneous
into the homogeneous,
reshaping the implicit into the explicit
and enlarging dictatorship into democracy
in the hunting of honey for all.
Otherwise, a glass of hemlock is ever ready
to give the last shelter
to the unfortunate speaker or builder.

Whenever You Embrace and Kiss Me

Whenever you embrace me
my angel in my soul
finds his greatness brimful
to make my paradise fertile
till the blooming of the last blossom,
and enchants you too to join on the floor
where I used to dance with my God.

Whenever you kiss me
my demon in my heart
feels the taste of your blood,
makes me hungry to consume you
till the end of my last supper
and mesmerizes you too to be happy
with the taste of my flesh and blood.

The Generous Darkness

Throwing the history in dustbin,
nowadays
I see you the best
in the darkness,
like your addition to me
leaving all sorts of
ocular and verbal intercourses
to avert the formation of hemlock
by our dogmatic attitudes
stimulated only in the sunlight
to write another love-story
with the nectar-
erupted in the smooth reaction
of our passionate action
held only in the generous darkness.

A Piece of Stone

In the eve of his death
a macro-conscious great man
repents throughout his sub-conscious journey
on the way to his final destination,
realizes his life-long sacrifices
as incomplete, so ineffective
in putting two and two together
to welcome a better sunrise for mankind.
Indeed, he regrets from his depth of heart
witnessing the presence of the dirty hearts-
full of garbage of selfishness and cruelty,
those are still left untouched and unwashed
though ever-skilled to pour hemlock
into the nectar prepared by him with great care.
In shame, he becomes a piece of stone
exhaling his last breath
and the people leave him alone standing
in a public place of interest beneath the open sky.

From Simple to Complex

A change in leaping and swinging
from the botanical branches
to the handles of buses and trains
changes the living equation-
from simple to complex,
where a singing stream
sinks into a roaring river voluntarily
compelling the pet-less cage
to be refilled with the wild predators
tempting the holy hymn,
"Live and let live"
to change into the devilish delirium,
"Hunt or be hunted"
bewitching everything for a change,
below the running feet
the soft earthen track
wears a rough blanket of granite sheet
and above the raising heads
the oriental sky still makes the golden sun
but with the declining carat of gold.

Longing For A Sweet Home

Maybe, quite enchanting,
yet all – the home seekers
ought to be careful of
a glance of glamorous eyes,
that composes a wonderful epic
in their hearts,
germinates some glistening globes
in the glossy sky of probability
and ensnares them
to participate in the fair of globes,
and ever-confused
in their selection and acceptance,
yet in the age of skyscrapers
everything is to be won
defeating one's own bad luck
or owning other's good luck
in the competition
of building a sweet home,
and the disciples-
both of the God and the Devil
longs for a sweet home to live
with the owners of those glamorous eyes.

Water, Air and A Life

Each and every
atom and molecule-
the architect of the earthly lives
look for the destination
set by an unknown autocrat
and make them mindful
to their own business.
Indeed, this is just a daily routine---
the sun rises,
and all plunge into the time-river
as water flows down
and touches the bottom
to penetrate it for flowing
down again to the deepest
hollow of the earth,
air flies up
and tries to touch the sky-
the ceiling of capability,
and wishes to pierce into it
to fly up again
to the highest cavity of the space.
Maybe, they are destined
for somewhere else
and for some other purposes
but a life can't flow down
or can't blow and fly up
but still it steals silently
the fuel from water and air
to enjoy an opportunist life
somehow in the world of hunger.

The Game Winning Kick

All of my sips
in drinking a fountain
may not be strong-footed
yet heart longs for a powerful kick
from the first sip itself
and a tumultuous celebration for the goal
achieved by the game winning kick.
Thus, a hilarious team of noisy sips,
boosted by a cartel of five senseless senses,
enters the field of longing by turn
to look for the chance to deliver
the most wanted goal- achieving kick.
But something wrong in the concept
That brings about the sabotage of misfortune
allowing the fountain to melt the sky down
and make the field slippery
and the kick doubtful too
in achieving the goal of a sporting life.

Anger

Within a fraction of a moment
it sets ablaze
the well-embellished paradise
built with love and care
to live with the dearest and the nearest
and can't be rebuilt
in spite of forceful injection of elephant
into ant,
yet it can be averted
at the very outset of its firing
compelling a frog to puff itself up
or a baboon to display its canines
or a man to puff his chest up,
stand tall, inflame his face
and look straight at the opponent
lowering the eyebrow,
biting the lips and flaring the nostril.
Oh my God!
It's an horrible expression of anger
that can be made innocuous
with the present of an earthly angel
as a third but most important person
in between the two wrangling demons
with a bucket of compromising hymns.

The Poor Heroes

Heroes are not made at all
rather they are born
to glorify their heroism with flying colours
for blooming a sweet smile at least
on the lips- abandoned and neglected,
yet, some heroes are born
on the unlucky thirteenth of a month
and compelled to be a titanic
in their every voyage for searching
of more gold to add to humanity.
Maybe they run towards the luminous sun
to inflame their torches of victory
but a black cloud chases them
the hint of a mysterious villain
to pour water on their flame of victory.
Indeed, they long for climbing the treetops
to entertain the leaves and flowers
but they are obstructed always
by the pecking crows and the shrewd monkeys
with their harsh crowing and chirping,
"Let us be entertained first".
Thus, pearls are cast to crows,
monkeys are garlanded under compulsion
and the sun sets in the rainy evening
before the poor heroes can climb up
to the stage of the waiting leaves and flowers.

Man is Mortal

In my soft childhood
my father, teachers and others-
all were hard in saying to me,
"Man is mortal",
I accepted
looking at the kite flying in the sky.
Now I am a confused adult,
made by one of my friends-
a scientist, a user of inductive process
in putting two and two together
for any brain-beating matter,
who regrets for all those unknown men
living outside his known orbit
far away in the caves of mountains
and the darkness of unexplored forest,
whether mortal or immortal-
just an unanswered query to him
and is reluctant to accept the proposition,
"Man is mortal"
and happy in hearing my clapping
on his thoughtful logic against the proposition.

A New Idea and The Watchman

To come to light,
a newly conceived ideal idea
seems to be scared and hesitated,
its unabated peeping
from the womb to light
for watching a through pass
leading to a benevolent home-
wherein a hidden reformer waits
to welcome and use it
in blooming smiles, in gloomy faces,
seems to be caused by
an undead robot- the watchman,
made of non-stick metal-
untouchable to any prayer or importunity,
standing just as an impenetrable wall
in front of the entrance
along with its ghostly gesture
and well ambidextrous too
in showing its reluctance to any new idea-
willing to enter the home
and to any sharp reformation
deserving universal sympathy and support
causing the raising heads and hands
against its own and its programmer's existence...

Playing a Cuckoo and a Cloud

It's a well-decorated stage
yet may not be beautiful
to all witnessing eyes
and all of us are compelled
to climb a flight of nine stairs up
to reach the compulsory stage
holding mother's kind hand
and cry in fear at the outset
of our deliberate performances.
Mother gets down
leaving us in the custody of two masters
one of whom
teaches us playing a cuckoo
to solicit the angels on the stage
who bloom blossoms in heart
and smiles in stomach
and the other
teaches us playing a cloud
to welcome the demons to come by us
who dance on the floors
of our hearts and stomachs
trampling the paradise
built therein by the kind angels.
We are programmed to learn always
as per our earnest interest
to perform our respective roles
tempting the tumultuous audience
to dance shouldering the heroes
and to throw stinky rotten eggs to the villains.

A Naked Hand

A naked hand
needs an impenetrable amulet
made of rhino skin
and goggles to cover up
its ocular confusions and hesitations-
the outcome of a dual duel
fought in its heart
between its limited ethics and unlimited wants,
to extend itself
near to a purse of someone else-
heavier than its own purse
either by uttering
the traditional hymns of begging
or by roaring
the thunderous dialogues of pillaging.

My Dream

Whenever I feel fit to shout at my miseries,
my two bosses are seemed to be diplomatic
in advising me on my miseries.
The visible one says, "every dog has its own day"
and invisible one whispers,
"God sees the truth but waits"
Hence, I cry hopefully,
"As the God can wait, so I can wait too
until my morning climbs down to my yard",
but before it gets down
a lustrous dream bewitches me
and makes me quite passionate to love it.
It is just my wedlock with a dream
and a solicitation to many baby dreams
to fulfill my dream for composing a family
somewhere in a dreamland
where I can work with no demand,
I can pray to the God with no hope
yet I wait only for the morning
when a dog or a man
will bark or shout at their respective miseries.

At Other's and Mother's Tears

She knows how to cast aside
one's passionate solicitation
and carry her point of reluctance
with a sweet smile.
Though she is my best friend
yet I can't see eye to eye
with her smile,
that sees off her refused boyfriend
and multiplies itself too at his disappearance,
with her prompt party with me in a canteen
where she looks as the happiest one
in her gossiping and laughing with me
and pulling the waiter's leg merrily
with her unabated making up,
with the new boys one after another.
that brings into play the same stories-
solicitation ,refusal smiling
and a party with me respectively,
but a new query in my mind,
"is she a stoic or a sick?"
Before I cut the link
with her hazardous company
I look her in the face and ask,
"How can you smile at other's tears?"
She looks daggers at me
and shout in her reply,
"They could smile at my mother's tears".

The Course of Journey

Nothing is to be dropped a veil over
the infinite depth of our heart,
millions dropping into it
seem to be a drop in the bucket.
Nevertheless, a journey is to be undertaken,
maybe, from a zero to an infinite,
in quest of necessity, comfort and luxury,
in guise of common devotees of
both God and Devil,
uttering the magical hymn "Something More".
In the vast course of journey--
plains, hills and mountains are trampled
by the haughty feet,
rivers, seas and oceans are steered
by the greedy hands,
elephants and whales are made upside down
by the commercial eyes,
ants and insects experience a combing search
by the hanging tongues and
the Hell and the Heaven are used in weight lifting
by the mysterious hearts
on the signal of the rise and the set of the sun
with many beckoning hands and eyes
of the nearest and the dearest.

Bearing A Grudge

Bearing a grudge-
a poor intention of a heart,
maybe, rich in good wishes
but ought not to be run down,
in putting two and two together
one can see eye to eye
with the mortals and the immortals,
"Bearing a grudge is sinless".
The morning –air-
free of dust and dirt
but not of grudges.
Temple, church and mosque-
the devotional catapults,
start throwing grudges
of all professionals and their counterparts,
wrapped with contradictory prayers,
filling the air and the sky with
the sound of the silent grudges,
"More please---No more please".
Ought not to be surprised at all,
even the prayer-loving God
forgets to make a figure
and stands in the crowd for a prayer-
full of grudges expressing His longings,
"More sorrows--- More prayers".

A Ladder, a Spear and a Beauty-Parlour

With a spear in hand
unabated has been my climbing
a standing ladder attached
to a hanging beauty parlor up above the sky-
far away, in the kingdom of clouds.
A universal hatred to my ugliness
made me untouchable to the wingless fairies,
boring to the hilarious hearts
and horrible to the dreamful eyes.

Dumped I was mercilessly so far
in a dark and suffocating room,
surrounded by the useless company
that my inability could arrange,
but could increase the degree of
obedience and sincerity to my heavenly boss
with humble prayer and importunity
for stepping up to the hanging beauty- parlour.

Successful I was to be blessed
and bestowed with a ladder and a spear,
since then my climbing has been on and on
to reach up to the dreamful parlour
for getting myself up-to-date
and the remaining chapters
of my unread and neglected epic collocated.
As I am blissful now in quick climbing
so effective my spear is to
remove the impediments and rivals.
Quite tension-free I am now
as I am accompanied by a blessed soul
and a hopeful heart in my efforts of climbing
up to win a place in the heavenly beauty parlour.

The Dogmatic Masculinity

At last, I surrender to the tradition,
fold my masculinity up
and posted it to my underarm.
Oh my God! What a magic it is!
Within a fraction of a moment,
my sky, my land and my beloved belongings
start dancing and singing around me;
my logical babbling,
rough and tough attitude
and "Do or die"---the powerful hymn
escape from my orbit.
The people,
sad, disturbed, angry and zealous,
owing to my free masculinity,
start reverse marching to their origin.
The needless eyes shut their windows down
yet they witness
the smiling faces, appreciating lips
and helping hands-
ever-ready for nurturing my newborn happiness.
The compromised heart
buys hundreds of charismatic worlds
in exchange for only one-the dogmatic masculinity.

The Poor Crowd

At Last, the poor crowd was made calm
in a mysterious night,
the witness-the moon was compelled to
hide behind the escaping clouds,
flushing a course of darkness in the sky;
an owl- the other witness,
sitting on the top of a banyan tree
sneaked, swinging the old leaves to shed down.

In the previous scene,
amid the encircling crowd-
hungry, thirsty, disturbed and agitated,
icy and hard was the mountain,
provoked the crowd to
set ablaze a flame of unrecognized emotions,
causing the melting of the icy mountain into
a few streams and fountains-
the blessings for meeting
hunger and thirst of the crowd.

Alas! The haughty mountain was merciless -
featured by devilish cruelty and destructive anger,
erupted fountains of fire and streams of lava
and engraved the poor crowd - hopeful for a new morning,
under the burning blanket of death in that cursed night.

Two Pictures

The laying of eggs by a cuckoo-
paints two pictures in our hearts,
one, a portrait of a dead scavenger
lying on a heap of garbage
and other is an image of a popular singer
who sings and poets compose poems.

The laying of eggs by a cuckoo-
sets ablaze the whole cage of heart
to gut off all the old tamed pets,
still consoles it with new seed that germinate
into innovated tree of greed
for the opportunist and shrewd.

The laying of eggs by a cuckoo-
causes the duel between optimist and pessimist
and sets us around the ring as supporters
to make the environment tumultuous round the clock.
Thus, we forget the death of the poor scavenger
and become blissful to the melodious singer.

Beneath the Shadow of a White Pigeon

A White Pigeon goes a long way in comforting a life,
hence, nothing can set its teeth on edge,
whether chewable or drinkable
and nothing is set aside by its blind call
in the compulsory gamble of fortune.
It likes to see eye to eye with all
who come to throw light upon their usefulness,
embraces all who want to be embraced,
ignoring the advice of its well wishers,
builds a skyscraper with the beloved friends,
nevertheless, antagonism rises and sets punctually
over its favourite skyscraper of friendship.
As an optimist, its moderate attitude
stands to reason always,
yet some odds are always taken into account
to set the tired logic at rest,
peace producing pills are used
still, controversies are conceived and delivered
to make a mess of the whole affair of a life
and compel it to make a mountain of a molehill
despite living beneath the Shadow of a White Pigeon.

Followers of Advice

It sets the teeth on edge,
and ablaze a fire in the eyes as well
yet the old advice is shameless
in persuading the innocent followers
to take time by the forelock
and make headway in life,
though ignorant to the negative role
played by a haughty bull
almost lunatic in running towards
and trampling down the enchanted followers
and driving them out of the way of destination.

The upcoming timid followers realize
the risk of taking a leap in the dark,
feels their hair stand on end
at the frightening body-language of the bull
and prompt to take their own heels,
saying, "Grapes are sour".
Here, an egalitarian can beat his brains
For a quick and sustainable solution,
Mingling the advice with power,
Inspiring and providing the followers
with amulets to be bold enough to
take the bull by the horns
making it compelled
to go back straight to its dirty stable,
bestowing the followers with sweet grapes
and fueling them to the brim
to make a headway in their lives.

A Heaven or Hell-No Problem

Lips and hands are tired
experiencing the oral and physical
hustle and bustle to climb up the stairs-
reaching the earthly paradise
built up beneath the cool shadow of nepotism,
protruded eyes are ever- cautious
in witnessing and realizing
the contradictory management of God and Devil,
inquisitive hearts are watching
a duel between optimism and pessimism
encircling the ring as supporters-
dividing into fresh hearts for optimism
and burnt hearts for pessimism.
Yet all are quite enthusiastic
to play their cards well,
they seem to be good players
in playing other false or a double game
and quite smart and prompt to the secret hint
of beckoning hands from the adulterated paradise
amusing the hearts even more than the divine paradise.
Leaving the hustle and bustle to hell,
the tolerant world is well surrendered to the flowing wind
as a vehicle to reach anywhere
whether a Heaven or a Hell- no problem at all.

Running in the Same Groove

Running in the same groove
sees eye to eye with the present
puts forth the same smile or the weeping-
enjoyed or suffered one day by the ancestors
and carried the same depth of feelings
through the capricious changes-
held in either sides of the path of tomorrow.
The sun, the moon, the stars and even the earth-
the permanent members of the same cosmic association,
found non-competitive in their non-stop marathon,
reluctant to accept a U-turn or a short-cut
or an unknown and uncertain innovation.
Keeping the pendulous minds under the arm,
the open eyes straight to the hereditary destination
and the stimulated soul ahead as a guide,
they run in the same groove,
collect the lying cards of fortune
and enjoy or suffer accordingly without any repent.
The lingering logic may break with the runners,
colossal hunger may lie down before to impede the race,
intellectual reformations and glittering innovations
may ensnare the dreamful eyes
and convince the heart to accept a change
or a U-turn or a short cut
leaving the same traditional path to destination
pushing down the life, character and spirituality
in the darkness of risk and uncertainty forever.

A Sweet Home

Maybe, quite enchanting
yet all the home seekers
ought to be careful of
a glance of glamorous eyes,
within a fraction of moment
that can compose a wonderful epic,
a comedy or a tragedy,
germinate some glistening globes-
outwardly similar and inwardly mysterious,
and swing in the glossy sky of probability.
Ensnared and confused are all
in the illusive fair of globes,
yet everything is sold and purchased
in quest of a sweet home.
Nevertheless, in the age of skyscrapers,
the disciples-both of God and Devil are still
looking for a sweet home to live
with the owners of those glamorous eyes.

Wonderful Kite-show

It's to be believed or not
but a human body is to be flown
like a kite in the sky
caused by the restlessness of brain
and its tumbling down to knee
making head blank and weightless
and body light to float in the air
in quest of something more.
It may be the sign of abnormality
yet eyes are indifferent to the symptoms-
reflected from the wonderful kite-show
exhibited in the open sky of hunger
where all go as they like
as hands start beating their own drums,
guarding their own ears
from the invasion of others' beating,
feet run faster than the mind
to reach "El-dorado"-the golden dreamland
trampling others' feet.
Heart hides again and again
in the pools of the clouds
and makes itself more mysterious,
but the old soul looks thoughtful and disturbed
before going for long hibernation
wishing "safe flying" to the floating body.

A Commercial Collision

A big poultry farm-
a small step towards self-employment
proceeded by three partners-
one is wakeful while others are sleeping
but they break their bread together equally.
At night, a greedy fox
moves around the farm
embellishing itself with a hanging tongue,
and looks for a weak part of the fence.
Oh my God! What a commercial collision
that the fox collides against the active partner
who was also moving around the farm
and licking the fence with his long tongue!
Very soon, tongue handshakes with tongue,
a whispering cartel is made active,
a secret part of the fence
is made weak diplomatically.
and the stock of chickens
start disappearing one by one
to satisfy the more and more
hungers of the two amazing shrewd and greedy.

The Two Suns

The burnt eyes
can observe a life in different angles
and perceive the illumination of the two suns,
one is ever wanted and so visible
while other is unwanted and hence invisible.
The visible sun is ever luminous
yet its light can't get rid of
the presence of that dark shadow
beneath which the synthetic goodness
of a compromising life grows up
and within a fraction of a moment
all are bewitched and attached
to live within the circle of that shadow
wherein they enjoy
their illusive days and dreamful nights
and assume their lives as satisfied and blissful
making themselves hidden, pretending and artificial
to one another.
The invisible sun is too luminous
to allow a shadow to cover its light
making all hidden, pretending and artificial
transparent and perceivable to one another
bringing them in front of their own mirrors
by breaking their dreamful slumber
and landing them from fantasy to reality
where dissatisfaction and irritation of practical life
bite them in every moment
and makes itself unwanted to the fantasy lovers.

Controversial Bath

In the dictionary of dreamful eyes-
owned by the adventurous teenagers
traceless is the word "illusion"
as to them all glittering things are gold.
My lustrous girlfriend- and me,
half- bloomed teenagers,
the owners of the same dictionary too –
attracted by the glittering water of a pond
to enjoy a memorable bath-
a bath of controversial nature
as prohibited for the teenagers.

As she leaped so I jumped
and we found ourselves in the mud.
Alas! An illusion was the water,
and fell again from the sky
as the water of the pond was evaporated
by the heat of our youth.
So what? Well featured we were
by chainless hearts,
brakeless passionate love to each other
and a thrill- loving and rule– breaking teen age.
Hence, nobody would stop us
from blooming a lotus in the mud
and we came closer and concentrated
on each other's naughty eyes.
One by one and step by step-
all events of the muddy game
were played and enjoyed enthusiastically.
Quite blissful we were in
leaping and jumping on the mud
and plunging into the depth of it
causing a bit of the mud to be
sprinkled in the air and in the sky.
Alas! The poor innocence
got a farewell from the teenagers
and in return a rough and tough adulthood
obtained a universal welcome and felicitation.

Realization

You licked and compelled me
to submit myself to you
as I was dominated and surrendered
by your passionate love for me
during your first stage of blooming
into an attractive piece of Barbie–doll,
deserving the wedding proposal of a prince
from a far world of fantasy.
Indeed, a lunatic time it was,
God's greatest gift "brain" was superseded
by an illiterate---half lunatic--- fully stupid heart,
made me ignorant to be hilarious
always in the luminous fair of illusions.

Blind I was to trust on your regular promises
before you're getting lost in my paradise,
you're blowing hot air into my ear
melted me down into a beautiful lake;
you're plunging into the depth of it
and your skillful styles of swimming-
snatched both my appreciation and solicitation.

Alas! The ultimate realization drew
the real picture of your character very soon
when the paints of your reluctance to marry me,
made me sad and ashamed,
filled my mouth of bitter tastes.
A hateful tendency of vomiting
resisted my comfortable respiration
at the change of a Barbie- doll,
into a mere fucking- doll.
The passionate tandem
suddenly fell into the deep of a dark pit
and I awoke up and witnessed the waiting of
a new and blissful day for me.
I came out with my whole entities
and felt quite easy to pronounce loudly
"Good bye, you worthless dickey-boy"!

My Girl Friend

Tumultuous was the last evening
and my vital life was cheerful to obtain
only seventeen candles to put off,
a bunch of hilarious hearts to add to
the garland of my sweet memory
and a silent and surprising
beckoning of an enchanting pair of eyes-
belonged to my girl friend –Pamela,
my best friend, not more than that.

A babbler she has been in general
but mysteriously mum she was in that evening
as something wrong in the ongoing party.
Hence my obligation was instant
to take her in a lonely and dark corner,
circumscribed her affectionately with
some formal questions relating to her
unprecedented role in the party,
but my inquisitiveness was unanswered.

A tiny smile appeared on her lips
and made me happy to push her to the hall
where all were quite blissful in dancing.
"W-a-i-t" her lips trembled but uttered,
she took my hand in her shivering hand
and looked at the floor
where she was engraving an unknown picture
on the tiles with her pointed shoe.
My second round of inquisitiveness
rushed to her,
made her lips quivering
and at last opened these up to pronounce
three most popular words
"I love You" by embracing me.
Surprised I was to her unexpected change,
amazed at wave of her pleasant emotion-
that had been bubbling up from her heart to lips,
made her different throughout the evening
and gifted me a beautiful tomorrow too.
Ensnared I was finally to admit her love
with a passionate kiss on her juicy lips.

A Paradise

The keen longing for a paradise,
maybe, a dream or a pet always,
but the sky alone is incapable and helpless
to germinate even a tiny flowering plant.
A paradise- a luminous and tumultuous garden,
full of blissful flowers and feathery singers-
exhibiting the colours and beauties of fresh life –
and singing the triumph of life as the best.
Paradise – assumed already as a belonging
of life-less heaven- a world of fantasy
but well appreciated and valued
only in the real world of blood and sweat,
well co-operated by open hands and hearts,
germinated on no-where other than the land-
Nurtured, enjoyed and glorified by the mortals
adding the sky to the land---fantasy to the reality
for a spontaneous intercourse -quite significant
for blooming a life in the paradise
and a sweet smile on the thirsty lips
as a consolation- bestowed upon by mother-nature
against the pains and strains of tough reality.

Diplomatic Eloquence

Let's feel, the magic of diplomatic eloquence-
exhibited during our action and reaction
as the traditional roaring- verbal or of arms,
chased to tarnish retaliation,
warned against unfavorable unity
and marched to trample the raising heads,
but amazingly all additions were equal to zero.

Fire, nevertheless, was alive
lying under the blanket of ashes.
compelled a set of intellectuals and updated brains
to combine together
dumping the arms,
and involve in hours of whispering
and counter – whispering
and at last agreed to produce the "Sweet Knife" -
polished by eloquence and sharpened
by all the goodness of gifts, rewards and awards.

Look, with in a moment, all toddling steps
join in a procession on the straight street
leading to the clutches of the diplomatic hands,
getting cut their throats of old hatred
with neither a wail, nor a repentance in
surrendering their future to the eloquent present.

A Kick

All sips may not be strong-footed
yet heart longs for a powerful kick
from the first sip itself
and a tumultuous celebration for the goal
achieved by the kick-
quite astonishing and game winning.
Thus, a roaring team of noisy sips,
boosted by a cartel of five senseless senses,
enters the field of longing
to look for the most wanted kick.
But something wrong in the environment
as an odour of the sabotage of misfortune is felt
allowing the noise pollution to melt the sky down
and make the field slippery
and the kick doubtful too
in achieving the goal of a sporting life.

Proverbs-Critically

Walking may be accompanied by a few leaps
on the way to the well determined destination,
but the proverb whispers and warns
"Look before you leap"---
the feet are chained promptly
and the world toddles in confusion and hesitation.

The blossom of charity may embellish others,
still one ought not to be unmindful to the proverb
"Charity begins at home"-
hence, home wins the first choice for collocation
as sweet is home with or without a dome.

Greed lays countless eggs of endless desires
but scholars and saints are serious in saying
"First deserve then desire"-
so, all pretend to be deserved shamelessly
and boost the degrees of their desires up.

A resourceful one spares something to nothing
yet the proverb reminds him the warning
"Give him an inch and he will take a mile"-
thus, selfishness wins the universal recognition
to practice for the welfare of own kith and kin.

A carping with upside down mind and brain
resolves everything into separate factors,
so he breaks the proverbs to find a critical meaning
and gives birth to a new proverb of interest
"As a goat chews all, so a mad talks all".

The Course of Journey

Nothing is to be dropped a veil over,
the infinite depth of our heart,
millions of dropping into it
seem to be a drop in the bucket.
Nevertheless, a journey is to be undertaken,
maybe, from a zero to an infinite,
in quest of necessity, comfort and luxury,
in guise of common devotees of
both God and Devil,
uttering the magical hymn "Something More".
In the vast course of journey--
plains, hills and mountains are trampled
by the haughty feet,
rivers, seas and oceans are steered
by the greedy hands,
elephants and whales are made upside down
by commercial eyes,
ants and insects experience a combing search
by the hanging tongues and
the Hell and the Heaven are used in weight lifting
by the mysterious hearts
on the signal of the rise and the set of the sun
with many beckoning hands and eyes
of the nearest and the dearest.

An Ensnared King

An illuminating and tumultuous evening
protrudes my eyes to a sudden attack on my fort
by a beautiful, lustrous and haughty princess,
only a sharp stroke of the amazing beauty-
blown on the steep dome
and my strong and almost invincible fort
built on my pride and contumacy
collapsed within a fraction of a moment.
The proud invader entered my fort
blowing her winning bugle,
snatched the throne away-
owned by my God so far
and pillaged the positions and the possessions
offered to my nearest and dearest.
She steered her magical rod
on my lips for uttering the passionate words,
"I love you my queen",
on my heart for a dance on her rhythm
forgetting all other stile and steps
and on my soul to banish it for a long hibernation
and started ruling my fort making me her king-
ensnared and lost in the invading fire of beauty.

Prayer of a Confused Life

Look, a life walks on carrying God and Devil
on either shoulder,
remains ever-confused and hesitant
as the inspiration and the temptation
both flow into the cavities of its sensation.

Feel the thrill of a tug-of-war
played between God and Devil
making a life as a rope round the clock
and pulling it towards them to own it.

But a sacred life is blissful and fearless
to show its back to Devil in bowing down to God
and pray generously from the depth of heart,
"Let our smile be bloomed on others lips,
a hut be built in others heart,
comfort be felt by the plaster on others wound
and a life be lived with all sacrifices
to compel God to smile on our lips".

It looks at the Devil and continues its prayer
"Let our selfishness be handicapped
in sharing the causes of smiles and enjoyments,
the flames of anger be extinguished
before humiliating the respectful and useful,
lustful passion be arrested with in a moment
before biting the soft skin of honor
and a life be lived with all cleanliness
to compel Devil to maintain
a million mile distance from a sacred life."

Double Standard Behavior

Our behavior ought to be pardoned
as compelled we are to make it double standard-
wrangler, babbler and savage in outdoor
and in indoor- peaceful, civilized and gentle,
in fact, a two- in- one mask is to be used always.

Quite prompt we are for wrangling with others
on the whistle of the angry outdoor situation
and making it more thrilling and thunderous
to flow out the hatred and anger of mind-
the spontaneous creation of the free situation.

Indoor, one acts the simultaneous roles
of three characters of blind, deaf and dumb-
the three toys of monkeys- the symbol of peace,
to collocate the drawing room with different gestures-
making the play on the indoor screen a super hit.

A consequent mental tug of war is on,
where the outdoor is defeated by the clever indoor
as the peace-lovers are destined to the addresses
of sweat homes to live like the kings and the queens
making the indoor untouchable to the lunatic outdoor.

A Poor Soul

A whimsical life longs to be on the floor
to dance with a haughty and naughty heart
and provokes the soul to enter the workshop
to arm itself with a sharp tooth set to bite
with a purpose of bringing the life on the right track.

The tingling of the flexible heart still continues
inside the dancing life on the modern bit
in spite of the presence of a biting soul,
yet more teeth are being added on the hint
of a noisy clock---attached to the divinity.

A keen discernment is added in life and heart
with up-to-date sagacity and black magic,
a plain appears automatically under the table
and pockets welcome the seas and the oceans
leaving propriety unheard outside the door.

The shameless virtue still peeps for a while,
throws away its useless plumb- line
and joins in the blind man's buff
to allow the lustre of wealth and resources
causing an eclipse on the rules and regulation.

Soul is made in heaven, so not to support-
pushing, pulling, pinching and at last biting-
all tactics are experimented serially to reform
and the vicious sight of the Hell is displayed in dream,
Alas, all seem to be in vain on the rhino- skin.

The nature's siren is on as a warning
to the unabated tingling, tickling and dancing
of a flexible heart and of a lunatic life,
the old Soul must opt for the last bite
though the teeth have lost their sharpness.

Me, My Smile and My Love

My smile and she- my love-
found together waiting
side by side and hand in hand,
keeping a distance from me and my dream,
deep - rooted in my eyes-
whether closed or open;
impose a painful separation to suffer
in each and every moment of lonely life,
float in between my dream and reality
and compel me to weep for overcoming
the frustrating distance.

A vast ocean of storm and stress-
it seems to my rudderless ship,
sinking down to the bottom of
death and destruction in any moment,
the fear- makes the distance unmeasured.

A colossal mountain of impediments-
it looks to my wingless life-bird,
falling down by a slip
near to affront and humiliation,
the probability- throws thrones on the way to her.

An oasis-less desert of multi-difficulties,
it appears to my thirsty eyes,
getting lost in the maze of
illusions and confusions,
the phobia- adds more miles to the gap.

Oh God, let my weakness
be visualized by her noble heart,
my compulsion be perceived by her sacred soul,
the distance be effaced by her proceeded steps
towards my poorness
and thus, a sweet conciliation be ensued soon
among my smile, my love and me.

Re-embellishment of Life

A gif picture of my weeping-
saved by the selfish separation
of my so- called sweet-heart
on the screen of my soft-heart,
turns me absolutely
monotonous to the hilarious world,
makes everyone - my nearest and dearest,
compelled to maintain distance from me,
sucks up almost the whole vitality of life
and now looks madly for a charger- for gaining
a lifetime recharge of my dying life
with a new flow of electrified nectar.
Before a coma reaches
and brings about a full-stop,
my life wishes to make
my suffocating inbox blanked,
protruding eyes normal to blink and look behind
and attached lips open up for prayers
to the rain to fall on my inbox
and wipe out the hazardous viruses,
to the sun to illuminate my heart again
with a tiny piece of its vital sunshine
and make my life charged up to the brim
and to God to bestow me with another chance
for re-embellishing my life again
with the divine ornaments of love, care and sympathy.

My Dear Coffee

My dear coffee,
maybe, from Brazil or Srilanka,
your invincibility started invading all countries
one by one and step by step,
winning the thirsty hearts of the communities
inhabiting all the world,
chamber by chamber- slowly and silently.

Air-conditioned you are by nature,
bestow the confused and tired with a relief
in extreme natural and physical conditions-
changing a hot into a cool
and a cool into a hot as per need,
enchant them to kiss you-
in return, you bring "a wow" on their lips,
compel every molecule and atom
the builders of human body,
to welcome your every wave,
ensnare them to swim in you
and enjoy a hot bath to be refreshed again
to continue their life-building function.
Oh dear coffee,
let yourself be ready for a change,
your present habitat in the top floor
be changed into an accessible floor
and an opportunity be given to the weak
to meet you, kiss you and enjoy you forever.

Blissful was the prevalent time,
so honest and innocent
as the people were;
they were made comfortable too
in rearing a pet--- an unadulterated trust-
a blind belief on
the powerful finger of the head
in sending all to a paradise,
earthly, beautiful and enchanting;
spontaneous to imagine
all eatables and medicines
as nutritious, effective and non-detrimental,
ascertained to rely on
the environment of the backyard,
filtered by the existing system of
learning and teaching,

embellished with a fair faith
in accepting atomic power as divine power
to bring about peace and harmony.
Anyway, the sun reaches the zenith
in the front yard,
makes the environment free of
mist and illusion
made people compelled
to be the disciple of agnosticism,
sneer their noses at
their head, food, medicines and miraculous power.
A girdle of peculiar darkness-
untimely and uninvited,
circumscribes the luminous people
while the sun still governs the zenith.

Development

Development – a vehicle of human civilization-
fueled up with ever-increasing hunger,
geared up by consecutive inventions
and destined to a procession of the hungry
irrespective of rich and poor
towards a permanent dining hall.

All are seemed to be greedy
in longing for something more
and making their lives
happy, happier and happiest;
enthusiastic is the vehicle too,
simultaneous pace is to be kept
to reach the attractive dining tables
soon ,sooner and soonest,
as if, an endless rivalry is in progress
between hunger and inventions.

Man and machines are ever- active
in assembling the parts of development,
polishing it to give a new glow and name daily
and enchanting themselves to exhibit
a lunatic game of blanking and filling-
filling and blanking again and again
in the name of so-called development.

Earthly Spirits and Fear

Quite wrangling time it was
despite of its old age,
even older than a grandfather
but golden was the moment with silvery touch-
not less than the hair of a grandmother
while two man-made spirits-law and punishment
fell in love
and took an oath to live together forever
in the witness of the rising sun.
A cool breeze of emotion and instinct flew in,
made the people pregnant instantly
and a chilled 'Fear' was born in hot mind,
ensnared them to be upside down
to shed down the black belongings,
the protruding eyes conducted a quick survey
of the borderline of dignity to look within,
the flying legs returned to their base
and started marching on the given track,
the long and sharp nailed fingers hid
in the safe- shelter of grip in hurry,
the night wings rooted out their blood- sucking teeth
and the ghosts joined in the hustle at the doors
of the saloons and beauty- parlours
to change themselves into the angels and the fairies.

Thus, 'Fear'- the blessing of the earthly spirits
solicited a cyclone and the evil–dirt was washed off,
with the next rising sun-
the ground floor was uplifted to the top-floor.

Of late, just a story it is to a grandson
who experiences a win in shooting competition
against an un-updated pair of spirits-
law and punishment
maybe, over-burdened with the stacks of ages,
and hence, weaker than the time of grandfather.

A Mad War---CIVIL WAR

An ocean of blood shedding
caused by external jealousy and enmity,
maybe, somehow endurable
but a motherland is speechless to console herself,
method-less to compensate her losses
and lidless in her eye-witnessing the destruction
caused only by the jealousy and enmity
among her own mad and selfish children.

Self-devastated now the mother land is,
experiencing quite helplessly
the colossal ambition of dogmatic characters
to attain the status of supremacy -
piling the dead rivals into a stack
to reach the level of abundance,
throwing millions of lives at risk
and thus bring about a dreadful
consequence---a civil war.
Motherland realizes the consequence,
and flies weeping from east to west
and north to south to save her children.
Alas! She cries out seeing innumerable dead bodies
scattered here and there half merged in blood
and millions of children are still in danger escaping to save their lives
to the neighboring countries,

Oh dear offspring of Noah-
the devotees of universal mankind,
come out of Ark, observe and realize
the pain that a motherland suffers from a foolish civil war,
listen carefully to the whispering prayer
that she leaves in the air
and follow the white cloud
that comes from the sky of that poor land
carrying the written message of her importunity.
Or, let us pray for the poor motherland
And reunification of her children and above all, a peaceful treaty among the
warriors that may cure up the madness of a civil war.

An instance of Divinity

Divinity –an unanswered inquisitiveness-
makes a theist mad in quest of a little hint
or an instance of extraordinary feature,
capable of resolving the mystery of existence
of a power- supernatural and paranormal,
building a faith to surrender everything-
pains and gains, to His safe-custody.
Indeed, cuckoo sings always in the flock of crows
and the record of common incidences may be added
and embellished by a celestial incident
as the amazing incident of a Vietnamese citizen,
compelling the atheists to stand in front of mirror.

A poor Vietnamese citizen---
a victim of self-devastating civil war,
an ill-lucky witness of the merciless killing
of his own beautiful wife and affectionate sons,
sneaked to the depth of the nearest jungle
along with his one year old baby son
and disappeared therein mysteriously .
The stony world remained busy
in moving towards selfish destination
and the tragedy of the Vietnamese citizen
and the others were simply forgotten.

Nevertheless, fantastic was the God's wish,
as the Vietnamese man was rescued along with his son alive
after passing of long forty years, wherein
human- surviving, indeed, seemed to be impossible,
yet they were found safe and sound,
as a miraculous power guarded and saved their lives.

Soul-blooming incidence it is for mankind,
quite influential and inspirational miracle-
as an atheist witnesses, perceives and realizes
the presence of divinity- a super power and the role-
it plays in each and every moment of our lives
and bows down to his super-natural power.
It is just another coating of paint, embellishing the universal belief of a God fearing
"Never be killed who is saved by God
and never be saved who is killed by God".

A Slap----The Slavery System

the tears of the headlines of newspapers
submerged the hearts of the sensitive readers
and they were ashamed of the news ---
"The existence of 36 million slaves in the world"
who earn and feed the shameless resourceful.
It was a slap on the pride of the babbling world-
claiming as modern, scientific and up-to-date,
climbing up almost near to heaven-
leaving behind the barbaric stains of centuries.
"Hunt or be hunted" was immersed in the deep of dark history,
"Live and let live" is chorused to worship humanity,
blissful we are to live a life and save a life,
moderate too to apply the virtues simultaneously
to the botanical and zoological welfare
and sincere to the messages of the divine messengers.

Nevertheless, something wrong in the air,
a sympathetic heart can realize the hidden weeping
that reverberates in the air and the sky
in the gap of tumultuous enjoyments.
Self-criticizers came forward and excavated
the universal body of mankind
and uncovered millions of hidden weeping faces,
empty hands and bare bodies full of black spots and stains,
recognized as slaves.

A heart-quake is felt by the humanitarians
and demolition of skyscrapers of civilization is witnessed,
caused by greed and cruelty to obtain something more-
a common ornament of uncivilized society of black history,
still embellishes some blood- sucking demons and Draculas.

Hark, the humanitarians! Let our invidiousness be elapsed
in recognizing the bloodsuckers,
our honesty, sympathy, kindness and benevolence
be stood against them with a collaboration of God's grace,
a new sunshine of freedom be illuminated
the future of the captive slaves forever,
and our civilization be decorated with the glittering
smiles of the slaves -rescued and rehabilitated.

Me, My Love and a Cuckoo

Once in an enchanting spring morning-
my monotonous mind experienced a change,
witnessed a climbing paradise down to my
abandoned garden shouldering a singing cuckoo
along with its botanical platform,
and the blissful flowers- dancing and flying
alternatively to the rhythm of the zoological song
and made me tumultuous too, in dancing and singing a welcome song.

Within a fraction of eye's blinking
my selfish teenage self expired and a young lover was born instantly.
Ensnared I was to the cuckoo forever
and generous to gift her a token of love
but she desired to own my garden only.
I was prompt in shutting my eyes
keeping outside all obstructive
hesitation, relations, rules and regulations.
In the name of love,
as I loved the cuckoo, so she owned my garden,
and the queen-less throne of my kingly heart.

Both became blind and bold in love,
could swim in the air to reach to the moon,
collected the luminous stars to gift to each other,
could race on the blue field of ocean,
played hide and seek in the undiscovered islands
and engaged ourselves to uncover
the mysterious wrapper of passionate riddles.
Indeed, the lovely relation of love with passion
makes us unmindful to the changing nature of the seasons and fate.
The sky was happy so far with its cleanliness
and air was so slow to flow in enjoying
the blooming of two hearts in earthly paradise.

Alas! A roaring of thunder in the far sky
made my Cuckoo scared of ensuing rainy season
she made herself free from my girdle
and flew within a moment up to the sky
in quest of another paradise
where spring is immortal and evergreen for lovers-
leaving me alone to wander in the lanes of memory.

Life Sings as Heart Beats

Life finds rhythm and sings
the songs of all seasons and occasions
and longs to be blissful equally in pains and gains
as heart beats to make life hilarious.

A fall into the eyes
of a soothing sight of earthly paradise
of botanical and zoological children
full of enchanting fragrances and colours,
makes life playful and it plays and sings too
as heart beats to make life tumultuous.

A sudden fall of the sky
on the collocated and fruitful present,
setting ablaze each and every thing
with devastating thunder and lighting,
makes life scared but careful, yet it sings
as heart beats to make life conscious.

A casual voyage in a new ocean
of beauty and passion with a lover,
plunging into the depth of endless treasure
and garlanding life with entire satisfaction,
makes life resourceful and blissful too to sing
as heart beats to make life adventurous.

A heartless hunting of professional exploitation,
oppression and humiliation to the last outcry,
witnessing the fall of one's image
into the furnace of earthly hell,
makes life sorrowful, nevertheless it sings
as heart beats to make life tolerant.

Hence, life sings and continues
until the last rhythm it finds from heart
and stops amid a pathetic chorus
when the stationary heart stops beating forever.

A Magnificent Painting

Blood sheds on the stainless canvas
turning it into the drops of sweat
and gives, thus, the birth of a magnificent painting
ensnaring claps, kisses, rewards and awards
to be generous to drop on it
from the blissful eyes and the perceived hearts.
Maybe, a bunch of blessings are also bestowed on it
by blissful and watchful aerial eyes
but a course of curses are booked
for those careless painters
who give their paintings just the beginning,
leaving the finishing to money and machine,
produce some so-called paintings-
lacking colour and scent of humanity,
dump them in the slums of garbage
and pollute the cleanliness of the environment
where the stainless paintings are still blissful
in picking the flowers up
thrown gratefully by
the dreamful eyes and the hopeful hearts.

The Statue Of Nelson Mandela

Nelson Mandela- the hero of South Africa,
expired, so free of earthly problems and tensions,
as expected,
love, appreciation, respect and gratefulness-
his earthly collections of heavenly powers
combine them together into a sculpture,
a giant statue of the great man
and salute again and again to his greatness.
A thirty foot tall statue
with arms outstretched
symbolizing his devotion to inclusiveness.
Alas! Death yet can't solve his all problems,
the witnessing eyes are poked by a pointed object,
an odd to the statue stands inside one of his ears,
blasts instantly the crowd in emotion
and circumscribes the environment in shamefulness.
A babbling bunny is witnessed,
tucked inside the ear,
brings about an instant demand
for the immediate removal of the odd
and an inquisitiveness regarding the definition of that odd.
Maybe, a by-product of the sculpting company,
Or, a wrong ingredient applied by mistake,
Or a side effect of paralyzing chilled death.

A Sweet And Soft Future

So sweet to hear,
yet a sweet and soft future likes to float
only in the lake of blood and sweat
as a sneaking young man
who waits by the bank of a border river
longing for a blissful world to compose
a sweet and soft future
along with his lustrous young lady love
and the new world of love and care
supposed to be discovered in
the other bank of the river.
Brimful the level of water
flows in and strikes against the bank
with terrific force and sound
and two pairs of proceeded feet
to unknown destination get wet,
and the whole entities get thrilled
but the young man is indifferent to all
watching the east and the west
and the cloudy sky too raising his
dreamful but thoughtful eyes,
the beautiful girl-the only companion
holds the right hand of her man
and comes closer and drives away
the black shadows of anxiety and hesitation
from the fair face her man of all time
and affirms those affirmatives
to remind him about the dreams
those they have knitted together
and the spontaneous swearing
that they have sown in the soil of their souls.
The young man and pretty beloved
look at each other and discover a trust
and a zeal to live and die together,
they look behind with controlled tears,
bade goodbye to the past
d plunged together in the river to swim across
in the quest of a sweet and soft future
which they must discover together.

The Carnival of Fire

The oriental fire
in the sky
sets ablaze
the stomach,
the heart
and the market
one after another
down on the land-
the regular events
of the carnival of fire
to turn the poor pocket
into ashes
and the eyes
into overflowing pools.

A Realistic Video Game

A realistic video game-
played on the screen of hard land
where every click may not be responded
and every level may not be crossed over,
yet clicking is always unabated
to make the kids hilarious
and the environment tumultuous
in moving a super hero
selected blindly by the blissful kids
but shrewdly by an invisible adult
to win each and every level of the game.
Slowly but steadily,
powers are obtained step by step,
villains are defeated one by one
and doors are opened level by level.
In the climax, only two doors---
almost twins and adjacent to each other,
remaining to be opened to win the game,
the left door---for the kids
and the right one--- for the invisible.
The blockhead kids---
quite blissful in directing the hero to the left door,
hopeful for winning the game
and prompt to press the click.

Alas! The hero is found irresponsive to the click
but spontaneous to reach
and open the right door in no time
on hint of an unheard click by an invisible finger
reverberating a blood-clotting laughter in the air,
making the kids frightened and disappointed too.

Treasures of Moments

A long procession of vital moments-
recognized as the vehicles
carrying the treasures of seven kings,
sets out a never ending journey
on rough and tough path of stony time.
A golden opportunity it seems
for the hungry crowd-
standing and waiting eagerly
to welcome, explore and goodbye the procession
in their respective capabilities and styles.

The mighty- mentally or manually,
plunge into the depth of the procession
raising their sharp weapons
and start their selective killing and snatching
to bloom fate-winning smiles all around.

Retaliation.

Amazingly, the ball is flying back to me
and compels my protruding eyes to witness
its dreadful spinning and speed;
and the haughty heart shrinks and realizes
a ruinous sequence is soon to ensue.
A few moments back…
my high-strung racket stroked
the ball and posted it
to the inaccessible address of the rival.
As over-powered I was
by my pride and contumacy
so was over-confident on my skill
and was over-optimistic too to obtain
the last achievement, the game point.
My body, mind and soul were prompt for
the hilarious clapping and warm felicitation
and blissful too in watching
the Samba of daydream around me.
Suddenly, a pin-drop silence paralyzes
the tumultuous environment
and I am back from fantasy to reality.
with astonished sensations
as the retaliated ball which is repelled
and addressed to a tough corner of my court.
"Oh God, please save my game,"
a bubble of importunity comes out of my heart –
almost haunted and blocked too
but inspires me for the last effort.
I tighten my loose grip, raise the racket,
jump over to the ball to reach beneath and blow.
My eyes shut their doors,
maybe, ears also reluctant to hear
the consequence of my last struggle for existence.

Two Languages

At night,
in our bedroom
all stories are seemed to be good.
Though my wife talks to me in two languages
and I use my ears and eyes to listen
yet nothing is there to handicap
our mutual understanding.
Very often I am amazed
at the contradictory longings of her two languages
as her lip-language hides the truth
while her body-language is so simple
to simplify the truth.
Though in the bed she embraces my lying body
keeping her face on my chest,
legs on my legs
and delivers her body-language
to pour oil in the fire
yet her lips say in drowsy tune, "Let's sleep early',
but I am prompt to justify
both her languages with love and care.

She and My Beloved Wife

On the way to return to my sweetest home
tired and exhausted,
a sweet passionate voice flew in my ears
"Have fun with me."
a commercial solicitation of a line-girl
with an erotic embellishment
and a youthful gesture of submission.
I had never been to their parlour
where injured and abandoned hearts
rush for a little plaster and shelter.
To my dormant lustful instinct,
it seemed to be a passionate summons,
or an inquisitiveness for a new thing
which slowed down my stepping ahead
and I stopped and looked at her.
Was it a miracle or the spiritual power
of a God-fearing who ruled in my
body, mind and soul
resisting any beacon of hell?
I looked at her
but witnessed surprisingly
the sacred face of my beloved wife,
on her face and those blue eyes too,
where my dreams bloomed.
A wave of shamefulness
floated my shameless instinct away
and rejuvenated my trembling honesty
to show my back to black passion.

Wedding Bond

The cool environment of past
used to project a sweet reality of life,
banished now in the dream land,
demonstrating a beautiful part of
an oriental wife,
collocating herself sitting
Under the Shadow of the Wings of a White Pigeon.
She was quite blissful
in remembering her beloved husband-
working in the cornfield
and combing a clean path in between
the two parts of her long hair simultaneously,
decorating it nicely with red vermilion
to welcome the Goddess of good fortune
to come along this path
and stay in her sweet home forever;
ever-wakeful for knitting a long plait too
to tie her husband with love and care
for a lifelong pleasant imprisonment
in her hot and sweet fort of heart
and ever-artful in soliciting the full moon
to come down to home to shine.
Walking along the path-
she combed and decorated already
to settle herself
in the mid of her lucky forehead
for illuminating herself and her cottage
to enchant her wedding bond.

Me, My Smile and My Love

My smile and she- my love-
found together waiting
side by side and hand in hand,
keeping a distance from me and my dream,
deep rooted in my eyes-
whether closed or open;
imposed, a painful separation to suffer
in each and every moment of lonely life,
float in between my dream and reality
and compel me to weep for overcoming
the frustrating distance.

A vast ocean of storm and stress-
it seems to my rudderless ship,
sinking down to the bottom of
death and destruction in any moment,
the fear makes the distance un-measurable.

A colossal mountain of impediments
it looks to my wingless life-bird,
falling down by a slip
near to affront and humiliation,
the probability throws thrones on the way to her.

An oasis-less desert of multiple difficulties,
appears to my thirsty eyes,
getting lost in the maze of
illusions and confusions,
the phobia adds more miles to the gap.

Oh God, let my weakness
be visualized by her noble heart,
my compulsion be perceived by her sacred soul,
the distance be effaced by her proceeded steps
towards my poorness
and thus, a sweet conciliation be ensued soon
among my smile, my love and me.

Death the Invincible

Let's look at the normal coincidence-
a hungry snake awakes up
and witnesses a foolish croaking frog
that brings the glittering of greed
in the sharp eyes and thrilling hisses of the snake,
"What a delicious dish!"
Within a fraction of a moment,
the croaking-box is swallowed up in a single bite
making everything silent as deep brine
with a merciless touch of chilled death.

Nevertheless, unabated is the human croaking too,
the babbling chatterbox is on
proclaiming their supremacy over other lives;
the exultant celebrates the victory,
building monuments commemorating it,
everything- below, on and above the land,
spontaneous to be arrested, controlled and regulated
for the fulfillment of non-controlled desires
and for their tumultuous celebration round the clock.

Let's feel the inevitable co-incidence-
the almighty death-the invincible
smiles at the stupidity of the Homo sapiens,
looking at deadline drawn by a mysterious hand
and spends only a leaping,
the millions of discoveries and inventions
loss their magical power of resistance
and finally the chatterbox becomes silent forever
making all the haughty additions equal to zero.

Time and Dreamland

Watch is ever fluent in uttering
a rhythmic tic-tac
meaning ' right time'
to knock the door of El-Dorado,
yet gossiping is on face to face

With someone of interest
adding wings to something precious
and allowing them to fly away
laying no eggs for us.
Nevertheless, the eyes are brimful
with the dream of the golden egg
and heart is restless in quest of its layer.

Look at the herd of horses
galloping and passing by.
So, what we are waiting for?
Let's start a hilarious race,
leaving the dead in the Hell,
jumping on the running horses
to ride them and proceed towards a fantasy,
difficult but accessible in reality.

Maybe, parasites crawl in hearts
tempting confusion, hesitation and illusion
to fall in love with our weaknesses
and set a journey out to nowhere
riding the wrong horse.
Let our consciousness be pinched
for killing the hazardous parasites creeping therein
and selecting the right horse to ride on
and rushing towards the beckoning dreamland.
Maybe, watch is still blissful
to reverberate its insightful tic-tac in the open air.

The Promises of My Diligent Day

Before it is dark,
my diligent day-quite sun-burnt and frost-showered,
promises to me to be cloud-free
to keep earthly god or devil in the dark
in accumulating resources
even beneath the luminous sun
and comfortable in keeping body and heart together
without the booking of a room in the heaven
knowing hell is available always to shelter
a man with horns and tail.

Vigilant to keep an eye on the finger
trying to have a finger in its pie
and another on the talking parrot
revealing even the colour of its under garment.

Careful in keeping
simultaneous pace with the running time
the best friend and master,
as a body guard
armed with a bow of two strings
to upset both the greedy finger and the babbling parrot

And independent depending on its diligence
to hold its head high above the sky
in absorbing the fluid of vice or virtue
and in justifying the earthly tag of war
fought every moment between the heaven and the hell
in molding up one more god or devil for them.

The Manipulated Heart

Tenacious, may be.
yet the heart is manipulated and compelled
to fold the outstretched arms up
and contented with a pinch-full enjoyment.

Secret parties- indoor or outdoor,
all are celebrated on the floor of meter-box –
well guarded by the hidden eyes,
cake, chocolate, chicken and car
all are well divided and enjoyed,
the hilarious extravagant and intoxicant
are not invited at all,
neighbours and friends are welcome
but up to drawing room only,
restaurant and tourist places are under-armed
and outing is confined only to the relative houses.

All are suffocating and painful of heart,
yet it feels good to the neighbour's appreciation
and recognition as a peace-loving family
but soul knows the dwarf hands
incapable to pluck off the prohibited fruits
hanging nicely on the top branches of abundance.

The Beginning of a Love Story

I never gave her smartness a cause-
a tiny opportunity
to break with my seriousness-
a synthetic mask
that could cover my shyness up to uncover
my heart to her
wherein only her name was engraved already.
It was a tumultuous evening of her birthday,
well featured by a candle light party,
many hilarious friends
and my well-known serious facial gesture,
she broke loose in breaking into my fort
and broke my ice
throwing her lips on my lips,
causing breaking off our hide and seek game.
I found a deep pool in her smiling eyes
to immerse my weakness and shyness
and allowed her love to break ground
in my lonely heart,
and thanked her with a return kiss
for breaking the neck of
the task of the beginning of our love story.

A True Scholar

He is a true scholar
who is ambidextrous in mingling
science and philosophy
to invent an earthly hymn
of meeting a purposeful end of life
and tireless traversing
from the top to the bottom of his capability
keeping heaven and hell
under the safe custody of his two arms.

Quite indifferent he is
to materialistic happiness and weeping miseries
living in the middle of inspiration and temptation
knowing the feelings as automatic and inevitable
to enjoy or suffer.

A well transformer he is
in extending the wings to fly in the sky
or swimming as a mermaid in the depth of black brine,
nectar or hemlock
both are welcome in their filter
made of appropriate reason and devotion.
and hence ascertained he is always
despite of hanging between
two opposite magnetic forces- the Heaven and the Hell.

Poor Honesty

Honesty
never hunts a blissful heart but it falls a prey
to a selfish attitude of a wild heart,
eats reluctant humble pie
along with its heart out
protruding its eyes to a duel
between its optimism and pessimism,
feels a resultant quivering under the blanket
as the three entities,
body, mind and soul fall, out among themselves
regarding the probable report of
post-mortem of honesty still alive somehow.

Nevertheless, they neither cut any ice
nor a draw a hard and fast line between
poor honesty and its grammar,
waste only their logical arguments one by one.

Maybe, honesty cries from the housetop,
leaving all hesitations and confusions,
for bringing itself to light
yet its divine virtues
draw blank to merge with the sun.

Hark! The offspring of Noah,
the remaining blossoms of earthly paradise!
Let honesty be escorted, respected and dignified
and be rescued it from the present danger of coma
before the jungle brings a full stop after honesty.

Alternative Healing Of Heart

The long-term illness of my wife
pours instantly a course of cursed ink
on my painting
painted efficiently and magnificently
with colourful paints
imported from my dreamland,
compels my three entities-
body, mind and soul to sink down to
the depth of bottomless ocean of fire
and snatches the fire-extinguisher too,
used in extinguishing my burning heart-
set ablaze by the evil attitudes of
society, profession, politics and religion.
Alas! The burning heart is helpless
and driven blindly towards the heaps of ashes
with no escaping reverse gear.
Nevertheless, my strong will power is bestowed
with a green signal
and I find myself submerged in the heap of
pens and papers
blissful somehow in writing something new
about my old misfortune,
my injured heart gets healed alternatively
by fucking white papers with colourful pens.

The Rhino Skin

The wrapping of myself with the rhino skin
makes me rough and tough and fearless
in facing the revolution of my boss around my loopholes
and buffering his jumping on me with his loudspeaker
speaking to my closed ears
steering his inflamed tongue
just tasted the hot breakfast prepared by his awful wife,
to extinguish his burning heart
by shifting the impact and the incidence of his suffering
to my shoulder,
already guarded by my impenetrable amulet-
made of rhino-skin,
by the grace of something stoic like the Devil.
At my home, I fastened the loop of the rhino-skin
as it is to be tested again for another inevitable round
by my family-boss
my beloved babbling wife,
rich in her complaints against my inabilities
leaving her each and every demand unfulfilled
and on my declining dedication to family
though I make myself a tolerant rhino-man
carrying my two heavy bosses with no complaints and groaning
In the evening, I put off my rhino-skin
and rush to a private heaven-
composed by a cartel
made of me and of my a few friends
the hunts of the same hunting,
where we convene a dance party
for welcoming the fountain of intoxicant amusement
to wash out all the humiliation of daily life
and to recharge all of us to endure the bosses again and again.

A Magnificent Painting

Blood sheds on the stainless canvas
turning it into the drops of sweat
and gives, thus, the birth of a magnificent painting
ensnaring claps, kisses, rewards and awards
to be generous to drop on it
from the blissful eyes and the perceived hearts.
Maybe, a bunch of blessings are also bestowed on it
by blissful and watchful aerial eyes
but a course of curses are booked
for those careless painters
who give their paintings just the beginning,
leaving the finishing to money and machine,
produce some so-called paintings-
lacking colour and scent of humanity,
dump them in the slums of garbage
and pollute the cleanliness of the environment
where the stainless paintings are still blissful
in picking the flowers up
thrown gratefully by
the dreamful eyes and the hopeful hearts.

Me and My Poorness

My poorness gets different reflections
from different mirrors
set in the eyes of my nearest and dearest
and hence different definitions are propounded,
conceived by their perceived hearts
and proclaimed by their open lips.

My father- my earthly creator
defines me as a mistake,
incorrigible during his lifetime
and shows his tired back
to the eyes of my dogmatic compulsion.

My dream-girl- the only rose of my thorny garland
repents for choosing me as her only man,
finds a similarity between
falling in my heart and plunging into a dirty ditch
and suffers from a sudden headache
in my passionate presence.

The government- my Godfather
endures me as an ugly black spot
on the forehead of my motherland,
non –erasable despite of a series of washing-
plans year after year,
and leaves me alone for automatic rectification.

My mother- my divine oasis,
bestows my helplessness with the shadow of
inspiration in my burning desert,
considers me with all her sympathy
as a penniless and compelled unemployed
and embraces affectionately my hidden tears and me.

The Poor Hand

A poor hand- quite naked and flexible,
needs an impenetrable amulet
made of rhino skin
and a goggles to cover up
its ocular confusions and hesitations-
the outcome of a duel fought in its heart
between its limited ethics and unlimited wants,
to extend itself near to a purse of someone else-
heavier than its own purse,
either by uttering the traditional hymns of begging
or by roaring the thunderous dialogues of pillaging,
otherwise,
within a fraction of a moment
its nudity will be caught by the fielding eyes,
the sores on it will be brought under the scanner
and the consequent humiliation
will be active to contract the poor hand to its origin
leaving even its own poor purse somewhere else.

The Compromising Metaphors

Whenever I go for an outing
I am blissful to go alone
garlanding myself
with a chain of magical metaphors
ensnaring me to think of my own shadow
as your hot and sweet company
made only of innocuous spices
creating
no logical contradictions,
no war of pride and contumacy
and no winning or losing consequence
though
those were held responsible before
for our foolish separation
from each other
and living somehow with the company
of the compromising metaphors.

Love in Earthly Style

True love is nothing but a ray of hope
reflected from the divine blessing
to someone else
well fortunate
to be luminous round the clock
and untouchable to any devilish project.
Nevertheless, an earthly life
spends its days and nights
observing or breaking the Laws of Nature
searching for all the things by turn
from a tiny needle
to a colossal excavating machine
making itself both illuminated and dark
as a disciple of both the God and the Devil
as per the demand of time and person
to comfort its needy and greedy
body, mind and soul,
becomes quite blissful
when someone appears in its life
in quest of a company for a while or ever
and the life needs too
to tame an enchanting illusion in heart
in the name of love
and it loves and is loved in earthly style.
Maybe, heart can feel
and soul also can perceive,
a needy and greedy earthly body
along with an opportunist life
can only trade but not love in its true sense.

A Heap of Mud

I played with a heap of mud-
well collected, refined and sterilized,
but still found useless for its restless wandering.
I shouted at the mud "statue" in synthetic anger
and surprisingly it was found obedient and playful too
in transforming it into a colossal statue
and enabling it to witness
the colours of all doors and windows
situated nearby or far away
and to comment on the running stories,
conceived and written in each and every moment.
Alas! The game was stopped
as the statue started melting by its own tears
and became a heap of mud again
making itself blind, deaf and dumb
to the weeping world as witnessed by the statue.

A Race Competition

A free race competition is being held
on a busy road
for winning a free ticket
to travel to "El-dorado"-
the golden dreamland
among three participants-
a fat cat-rider,
a horse-rider
and a poor foot-rider
who start using their respective powers
to win the race
on the blowing of the whistle.
The fat cat-rider
Runs, throwing money by the road,
the crowd on the road
jumps on the money
vacating the road
and the rider reaches the target first-
easily and comfortably.
The horse-rider
runs fighting against the force of the crowd
using his inborn horse-power,
takes his time to make his way
and reaches somehow the target second,
tired and exhausted.
The poor foot-rider
empowered by his only motivated heart
runs forward
but obstructed and pushed backward
by the dogmatic crowd,
he tries again to be forward
pushing the wall of obstruction.
Here the retaliating pushing
backward and forward goes on
and over there
the prize-giving ceremony is almost over.

The journey of a Coin

A catapult-
comprising of two fingers-
representing one's unquenchable lustful thirst
and his passionate crawling down
to many unexplored gold mines
incarnating himself as a tiger or a fox
tosses a coin up for a crucial journey
engraving him in one of its side
singing and dancing with the ensnaring fairies
and mirthful peacocks,
and leaving him alone in the other side
amid a dreadful ghostly desert
quite abandoned, ashamed, and injured.
In the course of journey
the uprising coin flies up to the outer world
as per general belief,
maybe, to the Heaven and the Hell as well,
consults with the authorities thereof
and then starts its inevitable downfall
confirming his fortune of tomorrow
and rushes down towards the land of reality
where he stands with his three trembling entities-
body, mind and soul
waiting for the unalterable verdict of the coin.

My Ocular Camera

My watchful ocular camera,
disappointed so far to the poking present,
longs for the course of a journey as a relief
to meet and shoot my ensuing tomorrow,
It turns behind,
plunges into the depth of my entity
and starts its travelling
and seeking something hopeful to shoot.

Finally my tomorrow is shot
and made captive in my heart
as an image of my tomorrow
exhibiting me standing on a stage
extending my empty hands to an angel,
looking at the sun
with a glittering piece of gold in hand-
engraving my name thereon
and thus my heart is filtered and polished
with in a fraction of a moment
to make me more tolerant to painful present
and more patient to ensuing fabulous future.

Your Cat and My Dog

I am ever cautious of the cat on your lap
along with its hidden claws
waiting for directing the duel
between your 'yes' and my 'no' and vice-versa,
but my compromised heart never calls for a duel
rather well ascertained it is
with the regular scanning of my heart and brain
to maintain an eclectic equation
that embellishes my eyes
with a sophisticated vision of verified tomorrow.
Maybe, my office-schedule tightens its grip
or my dog at my feet barks at your cat,
our evening tea-hour, nevertheless, is well trained
to extend itself to decade or more
provided that
your cat and my dog interchange their masters
and my eyes are fearless to kiss
your awesome fingers-
embellished with sharp and polished nails.

Something More

Our addition of something more and more
pulls instantly tongue out of mouth,
eyes protrude like ghosts
and compels us to respire so wildly
that make ashamed even a dog, a pet or wild.
The addition starts deducting the feeble
from the competition
trampling them mercilessly in the mad hustle
and piling them into a stack
to climb up to the level of abundance;
cheating the friends of same dish in sabotage
to circumscribe them in the cobweb of bankruptcy,
killing the rivals in conflict
to fuel and exercise its monopoly power
and tempting the God fearing to go under the devil
to worship it and gain its black blessings.

The addition flies, smokes, and greed up and up
with sharp nails of carbon and desires
to pinch the ozone layer in the sky
and leak our hearts
to bid goodbye to oxygen and life
from the body of ozone layer and mankind respectively.

Two Neighbours

At night,
time starts steering the magical stick,
to make the hilarious houses unconscious
from the huts to the skyscrapers-
shutting their doors and windows
but enchanting the two shrewd neighbours,
who express their concealed friendship through hotline,
organize luxurious party in a secret paradise,
exchange surprise gifts and packages
and discover the tactics of making people fools.

Routine and wise, the sun appears in the morning,
and makes everything from material to immaterial
transparent and comprehensible
to open eyes and ears and to hearts and souls
making the two clever neighbours to wash out the friendship,
proclaim hostility in front of microphone,
throw the bombs to each other
made of synthetic hatred and anger,
inject the alcohol of enmity in to people's minds
and build up an aggressive and toddling society.

Within a fraction of a moment-
universal friendship and fraternity get mingled,
peace and harmony commit suicide,
intelligence and intellectuality hide in the knees
and all fools join in well-planned hustle and bustle
on the top floor and in the ground floor-
cheating, pillaging, and even blood shedding.
Alas! The earth rotates and again night appears,
brings the two neighbors lips to lips through cell phone
and in the outside a pathetic weeping reverberates in the air.

A Stranger

Always unpleasant, unsolicited and unnoticed too,
yet it dares to break the girdle quite silently
and trespass the lanes of our lives,
Interfering all work---performed with cares
all the ways---chosen with justification
and demeans the contributions---made with sacrifices.

It traverses all quarters and looks for something,
shrivels its nose as something wrong therein
and comments proudly with irritating gesture.
and pushes us instantly in the laboratory
where the virtues of tolerance and patience are to be tested
under the scanners round the clock.

Men with dieting hearts and tourist brains mingle mingle
react and set ablaze their creations,
breakables are mingled in a moment and flown away
and soluble are diluted instantly and washed away.

But men with rhino-skin and brimful tolerance and patience
recognize and accept the unwanted stranger as a teacher
endure his finger pointed towards the dirt of weakness
and sweep them out of life to gain a neat and clean future.

The Poor Crowd

At Last, the poor crowd was made calm
in a mysterious night,
the witness-the moon was compelled to
hide behind the escaping clouds,
flushing a course of darkness in the sky;
an owl- the other witness,
sitting on the top of a banyan tree
sneaked, swinging the old leaves to shed down
on the pathetic story of the encircling crowd-
hungry, thirsty, disturbed and agitated,
around an icy and hard mountain,
who set ablaze a flame of unrecognized emotions
expecting the melting of the icy mountain
into a few streams and fountains for meeting
their century long hunger and thirst.

Alas! The haughty mountain was merciless -
featured by devilish cruelty and destructive anger,
erupted fountains of fire and streams of lava
and engraved the poor crowd – hopeful for a new morning
under the burning blanket of death in that cursed night.

My Guests

My guests are ever-solicited
yet they cross me daily
flying over my raising hands
or running behind my hopeful eyes
showing their selective nature.
Yet, my thirsty eyes
get quenched one day
as my guests are witnessed
entering my poor parlour
walking on the way
built up by my sweat and blood
steering their magical rods
on me and my poorness
to make my heart brimful in emotion
and lips flexible
to blast together a musical laughter
and feet hilarious in joy
to show their dancing steps
Alas!
As time passes,
so the guests start disappearing
in the bottomless holes of my booster,
boosting my unaccounted
smile, laughter and dancing up.
My experienced heart gets a lesson
to install a rationing system of amusement,
boosted up by a new booster with a regulator
and waits for the arrival of new guests again.

The World and the Wiseacres

In the kingdom of wiseacres
wisdom is made captive
and dignified as their own property
and all are automatic to be bewitched
in the use of it
in blind chasing and counter-chasing
of one another
as my sister's wit chases me,
my brother's wit bites me
and my friend's wit barks at me
since my wit makes them foolish
forgetting the chained wisdom-
weeping for its freedom
in the composition of a benevolent epic-
an immortal inspiration to mortal mankind,
but to the wiseacres –
the owners of snake- ears,
the woeful importunity is nothing more than
a tasteless vibration in the air
that can be left unheard.
Nevertheless, the earth rotates and revolves
and the world gives indulgence to wiseacres
acting the roles of deaf, dumb and blind
in the rescue operation of the captive wisdom
from the clutches of the mad wiseacres.

An Old Lovebird in Modern Times

A homeless old love bird
still cries and dies today for a nest-
an old fashioned heart of its own time
built and embellished
with all its cardinal virtues
though outdated to an updated heart
that raises its nose at the lovebird
and babbles in a tomboy style,
"It's the modern time
my dear old lovebird,
an off-season for heart hunting
by the traditional emotions and feelings,
rather a reasonable time to adopt a duck-bath-
featured by water-proof plunging and swimming
keeping the lazy emotions in the custody of underarm"

Two Tongues

Wonderful maybe,
but I got a pair of tongues-
set by my birth and profession.
to simplify the jumbled lanes of my heart to others,
and restrict a critical estimation too,
made by their similarity and difference
from each other
as both stand hand in hand
in spraying honey and clustered oil,
in the ears of the friends and foes,
though in location
they are separated by five oceans,
in emotional expression.
If one is babbler
then the other is little stammerer
and in ethical justification
communal is the tongue by birth
and universal by profession the other.
Well disciplined these are
in maintaining a line of control and jurisdiction
as in the outdoor
my hands are outstretched to embrace the universe
and the professional tongue,
forgetting all jealousy and hatred
wishes to be loud in uttering,
"I Love You",
but in the indoor,
quite spontaneous and communal I am
using my tongue by birth
to express my love to my beloved wife,
"Aami Tomake Bhalo Bashi",
an oriental expression of love,
meaning the same- I Love You.